A Farewell to
STEAM

Tony Butcher

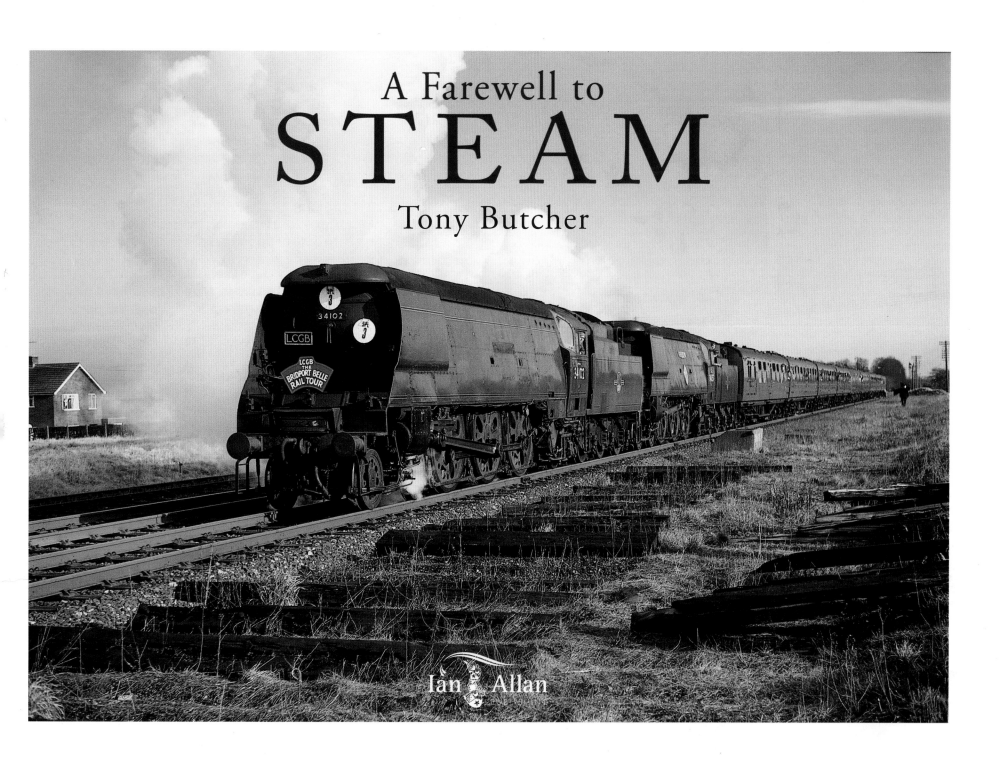

Ian Allan

Front cover: Immaculate in restored condition, preserved 'Castle' No 4079 *Pendennis Castle* storms past Pulford, south of Chester, on 4 March 1967 with the 'Birkenhead Flyer' — the first of the Ian Allan specials commemorating the GWR route from Paddington to Birkenhead. This was to be the locomotive's last outing before it was sold to a mineral railway in Australia. It has since been repatriated and is now being returned to working order.

Back cover: Immaculate 'S15' 4-6-0 No 30837 approaches Bentley station with the first of the LCGB 'S15 Commemorative' railtours on 9 January 1966. At Bentley 'U' No 31639 took over to run down the branch to Bordon and back. Afterwards the 'S15' continued to Eastleigh shed before returning in the dark to Waterloo. The Bordon branch had been freight-only since 16 September 1957, but it offered a northern connection with the Longmoor Military Railway.

Previous page: A pair of unrebuilt Light Pacifics — Nos 34102 *Lapford* and 34057 *Biggin Hill*, pull away from a photo-stop outside Grateley station *en route* to Salisbury with the LCGB 'Bridport Belle' railtour of 22 January 1967. A leading member of the LCGB was known to have a penchant for double-headed unrebuilt Bulleid Pacifics, a sight never normally seen on the Southern main lines. By now these locomotives were among the last seven unrebuilt Light Pacifics still in service. No 34102 *Lapford*, indeed, was the last unrebuilt Pacific to work a normal service, on the 6.44am Salisbury–Waterloo on 5 July 1967.

First published 2010

ISBN 978 0 7110 3480 8

© A. R Butcher 2010

Published by Ian Allan Publishing

an imprint of Ian Allan Publishing Ltd, Hersham, Surrey, KT12 4RG

Printed in England by Ian Allan Printing Ltd, Hersham, Surrey, KT12 4RG

Code: 1008/B1

Distributed in the United States of America and Canada by BookMasters Distribution Services

Visit the Ian Allan Publishing website at www.ianallanpublishing.com

Mixed Sources
Product group from well-managed forests and other controlled sources
www.fsc.org   Cert no. SGS-COC-005526
© 1996 Forest Stewardship Council
FSC

List of abbreviations

BLS	Branch Line Society
BR	British Railways
CR	Caledonian Railway
DNS	Didcot, Newbury & Southampton
GNR	Great Northern Railway
GNSR	Great North of Scotland Railway
GWR	Great Western Railway
HCRS	Home Counties Railway Society
LYR	Lancashire & Yorkshire Railway
LBSCR	London, Brighton & South Coast Railway
LCGB	Locomotive Club of Great Britain
LMR	Longmoor Military Railway
LMS	London, Midland & Scottish Railway
LNER	London & North Eastern Railway
LNWR	London & North Western Railway
LSWR	London & South Western Railway
MGNJRS	Midland & Great Northern Joint Railway Society
MRTS	Manchester Railway Travel Society
NBR	North British Railway
NCB	National Coal Board
NELPG	North East Locomotive Preservation Group
NER	North Eastern Railway
PBA	Port of Bristol Authority
RCTS	Railway Correspondence & Travel Society
REC	Railway Enthusiasts' Club
RPS	Railway Preservation Society
RSS	Railway Society of Scotland
SDJR	Somerset & Dorset Joint Railway
SCTS	Southern Counties Touring Society
SDJR	Somerset & Dorset Joint Railway
SLS	Stephenson Locomotive Society
SMJR	Stratford-upon-Avon & Midland Junction Railway
SR	Southern Railway, Southern Region
SVRS	Severn Valley Railway Society
WRS	Warwickshire Railway Society

INTRODUCTION

My early boyhood interest in railways centred on steam locomotives themselves, and I remember a few visits with a friend and his father to locomotive works such as Eastleigh. My attention then turned to model railways and the obligatory Hornby Dublo train set. Some years later, however, a cousin of 13 came to stay for a week. He, like his father and brother, was mad on railways, both model and full-size. To keep my young visitor occupied during the week I took him up to Clapham Junction to do some train-spotting, and my interest in the real thing was reawakened. I did then actually start collecting numbers in the 1955 Ian Allan 'ABC', but I had also been given a basic camera for my birthday, and I began taking a few black-and-white photographs. However, the camera was severely limited by having a maximum shutter speed of ⅟₇₅sec. The following year (1956) I graduated to a 2¼ × 3¼ Kodak camera with a ⅟₂₀₀sec shutter, and started to take my first reasonable photographs.

My action photography started at Surbiton (in those days you could see the whole 'Lord Nelson' class in a day, unless one happened to be in works) and along the North Downs on the Redhill–Reading line. Not yet having a car, I had to travel by public transport and walk the rest. The Redhill–Guildford line still had the last of the SECR 'D'-class 4-4-0s running along the North Downs, as well as the odd 'T9', 'Q', 'Q1' etc, in addition to the ubiquitous Southern Moguls. In addition there was a daily Western Region working from Reading and back, initially a '43xx' 2-6-0 and later a 'Manor' 4-6-0, and on many mornings I managed to slip from my workplace in Redhill or Dorking to photograph it. On summer Saturdays there were also through trains from the Midlands to the South Coast.

A further period followed during which I took black-and-white shots of everyday steam, within the limits of not having my own transport and studying at university. By this time I had graduated to an Agfa Isolette 2¼ square camera with a ⅟₅₀₀sec shutter. It was a good little bellows camera, but it did suffer from some drop-off in definition on the left-hand side at larger apertures. My highlight of those days was a summer Saturday spent on the South Devon banks in 1957, when in an endless stream of trains all but one was double-headed, hauled by every possible combination of GWR 4-6-0s, even including double-headed 'Kings'.

At this point, I met a certain girl who later became my wife. What with courting, buying a house and my job, this effectively put a stop to my railway activities for three years, to my lasting regret — from a railway point of view, I hasten to add.

I did manage to start photographing steam engines again on my honeymoon in Cornwall in 1961, and I got my first introduction to steam in the North East, for that was where all my wife's relatives came from. I was still taking black-and-white pictures. I did not start taking colour pictures until 1962, and they were 2¼in-square format colour negatives and transparencies taken with a very basic Kodak camera belonging to my wife.

It was not until mid-1963 that I started taking 35mm colour transparencies; by then the Beeching report was starting to take effect, and many of the locomotives were dirty and unkempt. Furthermore, many of the famous classes (*e.g.* 'King', 'Princess Royal', 'Schools', 'Lord Nelson', 'King Arthur', unrebuilt 'Patriot') had been fully withdrawn at the end of 1962. My photographic interest then turned more and more to special railway enthusiasts' tours, for which locomotives were normally very well turned out and were often the last survivors of classes that could by then be seen only with difficulty if at all in normal service. My holiday leave in those days was severely limited to three weeks and had to include my wife's holidays; that almost all these specials ran at weekends was therefore a big plus.

Often, of course, the weather was not good, and efforts to capture the shots on 50ASA Agfa colour transparency film were not always successful.

Left: GNSR 4-4-0 No 49 *Gordon Highlander* (BR Class D40 No 62277) backs down on to Edinburgh St Margarets shed, having headed the first part of the SLS/BLS 1965 'Scottish Rambler' from Glasgow via Edinburgh Waverley to Leith Central on 19 April 1965.

I continued taking black-and-white shots up to the end of BR steam, initially on 35mm FP3 film and latterly on 2¼in square FP3 and 400ASA TRIX, the latter much the more useful in dull weather; on account of its low speed rating 35mm 25ASA Kodachrome film was usually used only in summer weather, which naturally limited my coverage of these enthusiasts' railtours in colour.

The running of special steam-hauled railtours for railway enthusiasts dates back at least to 1938, when the GNR Stirling 'Single', brought out of retirement by the LNER for 'Flying Scotsman' publicity, was used by the Railway Correspondence & Travel Society for a run to Peterborough. Since then many steam specials have been run, more than 500 in the final 20 years of BR steam alone. But there was only a relatively thin sprinkling of such tours until the early 1960s, when the enthusiasts' special blossomed to full flower, only to die in a final blaze of glory in the summer of 1968 at the end of steam on British Railways.

These railtours were run by various different enthusiast societies, which showed considerable resource and ingenuity in choosing interesting itineraries allied to varied motive power. Inevitably one must mention the 'big three', which had run well over a hundred tours each by the end of 1968, namely the Railway Correspondence & Travel Society, the Stephenson Locomotive Society and the Locomotive Club of Great Britain.

A good steam tour had many attractions, all concentrated into the few hours available. The routes chosen, often circular in nature, were usually of particular interest, traversing little-used cross-country lines, freight-only branches and many other delightful branches of the pre-Beeching type. On occasion the tour's itinerary was chosen to coincide with the last rites on a particular branch line or cross-country route, several of them on or near the last day of normal BR operation. The interposed fast main-line stretches were, of course, of interest and sometimes exciting, but to me the greatest pleasure came from meandering along some secluded country line, with frequent stops for water, photographs or locomotive manoeuvres, or just to wander round. Many may disagree, but this is a minor failing of today's preserved steam specials, fine though the big engines look as they race past.

Numerous choice memories of these steam railtours stay in my mind from over the years: the flat-out assault of 'Castle' No 7005 *Sir Edward Elgar* on Sapperton Bank in the Cotswolds in the gathering dusk with sparks flying heavenwards (which later resulted in frequent stops to recuperate and regain steam pressure); the preserved Caledonian Single almost slipping to a stand in a raging blizzard on the 1-in-50 climb up Glen Ogle yet somehow managing to continue and struggle up to Killin on its single drivers; the two petite Beattie well tanks gleaming in the sun at Surbiton on their last outing, and then nearly having to drop their fires at Hampton Court and wait until the local fire brigade arrived in the nick of time; the thrill of waiting out in the wilds for a sparklingly clean locomotive on a steep climb, and finally hearing its roaring beat and seeing it storm round the curve below. On occasions there were big disappointments, as when I went to photograph the last Great Eastern 'B12' 4-6-0 on the climb out of Blisworth on the line to Northampton only to find that I was on a mineral line to a quarry nearby and not the BR line; but I heard the 'B12' roaring past and saw its trail of heavy black smoke, only a short distance away!

The 'Scottish Rambler' tours of the 1960s, on which I first travelled in 1963 and which I chased by car in 1965, is another that holds special memories for me, and to this day I still hope to see again, working, at least one of the four Scottish preserved locomotives long incarcerated in the museum in Glasgow — what a shame that has been!

One could, of course, go on for ever, but such to me are the memories of these special tours. This volume can contain only a small selection from my collection of photographs taken over the last years of steam, but I hope they portray something of the attraction and fascination that these steam specials certainly held for me then, and increasingly in later years, I believe, for many others.

Tony Butcher
Crawley Down, Sussex
July 2010

SOUTH CENTRAL

Left: A pair of very well turned-out LBSCR tanks — diminutive Class A1X 'Terrier' No 32636 and a much bigger 'E6' 0-6-2T, No 32418, pause for water at Lewes with the RCTS 'Sussex Special' of 7 October 1962, which they had headed from Brighton. To the right the platform curves away to serve the lines to Eridge and beyond, as well as the 'Bluebell' line before its closure. After Lewes the train proceeded to Seaford; the locomotives subsequently went on shed at Newhaven. No 32418 was condemned in December 1962, but No 32636 (the oldest locomotive on BR, having been one of the first batch of six, which appeared in 1872) saw out its time on the Hayling Island branch until its closure on 2 November 1963, and was then acquired by the Bluebell Railway. The tour had started at London Bridge and was headed to Brighton by 'Schools' class 4-4-0 No 30925 *Cheltenham*. All the 'Schools' were withdrawn at the end of 1962, the very severe winter of 1962/3 precluding the running of a commerorative special. *Cheltenham* is preserved in the National Collection but is not currently in working order).

Above: Light Pacific No 34066 *Spitfire* prepares to leave Tunbridge Wells West with the RCTS/LCGB 'Sussex Downsman' railtour of 22 March 1964, which it would head down the 'Cuckoo line' via Eridge to Pevensey, where Class N Mogul No 31411 would take over for a visit to Lewes (East Sidings) and, after reversal, on to Brighton. *Spitfire* was the locomotive involved in the Lewisham disaster of 4 February 1957. The impressive station layout and buildings marked the original limit of the LBSCR lines. The main station building is now an hotel, and the station layout has been cut back to a single track alongside the engine shed on the left, which survives as the headquarters of the Spa Valley Railway.

The last operational Drummond 'M7' 0-4-4T, No 30053, waits in the siding at Caterham to take over the LCGB 'Surrey Wanderer' railtour from Standard 2-6-0 No 78018 on 5 July 1964. The 'M7' took the train up the branch to Purley and then visited the Tattenham Corner branch. General withdrawal of the 'M7' tanks began in 1957, but a few soldiered on until 17 May 1964, by which time they were confined to the Lymington and Swanage branches. No 30053 was specially reinstated for one day only to work this special, beautifully turned out for the occasion by Nine Elms shed. After being exported to the USA, it has now returned to active service in the UK on the Swanage Railway.

After arriving at Tattenham Corner terminus the 'M7' shunts its stock out of the station in order to run round the train, before returning to Victoria with a diversion to Kensington Olympia *en route*. For locomotives built between 1887 and 1911, with no significant alterations over the years, the 'M7s' enjoyed a remarkably long career.

HAMPSHIRE BRANCH LINES (1)

Left: The SCTS 'South Western Limited' railtour is seen at Fullerton Junction on the branch line from Andover Junction through Stockbridge to Kimbridge Junction behind a nicely turned-out Drummond '700' 0-6-0, No 30309, one of the last survivors of the class — nicknamed 'Black Motors' — from Salisbury shed. The locomotive hauled the train from Salisbury to Eastleigh, where the last active 'King Arthur' 4-6-0, No 30770 *Sir Prianius*, took over for the evening run back to London on 2 September 1962. This tour was also the last special run by a 'Lord Nelson' 4-6-0, No 30861 *Lord Anson*, to Exeter, and marked the end of these two fine classes in use on British Railways. Fortunately a survivor of each class is preserved in the National Collection.

Below: Q1'-class 0-6-0 No 33006 was well turned out for the LCGB 'New Forester' railtour of 19 March 1966. Here it is seen backed on the train at Totton, after a trip down the Fawley branch with two 'USA'-class tanks, and will now head the train to Brockenhurst and Lymington Pier. Nos 33006, 33020 and 33027 were the last 'Q1s' in service. All had been withdrawn in January 1966, but No 33006 was reinstated for special workings until April of that year.

SR 'USA'-class 0-6-0Ts Nos 30064 and 30073, both in BR lined green, run back up the Fawley branch in a sylvan setting near Marchwood with the RCTS 'Solent Limited' railtour of 20 March 1966. By this time both locomotives were being used as shunters at Eastleigh Works. This tour started from Waterloo behind 'Battle of Britain' Pacific No 34089 *602 Squadron*, which hauled the train as far as Salisbury. Standard Class 4 No 75070 then took it on to Southampton Ocean Terminal, where the two 'USAs' took over as far as Fawley, before No 75070 hauled the train again to Fareham. Here Class U 2-6-0 No 31639 took over for a short trip down the freight-only Gosport branch, before both locomotives then double-headed the special back to Waterloo.

SOMERSET & DORSET

Right: Somerset & Dorset '7F' 2-8-0 No 53808 (evidently given a special clean by cleaners at Bath (Green Park), halts at Shepton Mallet in the late afternoon sun with the LCGB 'Somerset and Dorset' railtour of 30 September 1962 *en route* to Bath (Green Park), having covered the whole length of the SDJR from Broadstone Junction. Six of this class of 11 had already been withdrawn, but No 53808 was destined to be preserved and is now in working order on the West Somerset Railway. This tour had an excellent itinerary, starting at Waterloo behind a Light Pacific and using the Brockenhurst–Ringwood line to reach Broadstone. A trip was made up the Highbridge branch behind a GWR 0-6-0, seen opposite. On arrival at Bath a SDJR '4F', No 44558, took over for the run to Bristol, where one of the last ex-GWR '47xx' 2-8-0s, No 4707, took over in the gloom for the run back to London. Unfortunately the '47xx' failed near Swindon, and a Hawksworth 'County' had to be summoned to rescue the train.

Below right: The LCGB 'Somerset and Dorset' railtour of 30 September 1962 waits to leave Highbridge, on the SDJR branch from Evercreech Junction, behind GWR '2251' 0-6-0 No 3210, in BR lined green. By now the '2251s' had become quite common on the SDJR. On this occasion No 3210 had already headed the train down the normally disused end section of the branch to Burnham-on-Sea. The train was then rejoined by SDJR '7F' No 53808, for the onward journey to Bath.

Far right: A pair of Ivatt 2-6-2Ts, No 41307 leading No 41283, prepare to leave Glastonbury after a photo-stop with the LCGB 'Mendip Merchantman' railtour on a trip down the SDJR Highbridge branch from Templecombe, on 1 January 1966. After Glastonbury poor weather, as well as the early sunset that was only to be expected at this time of year, made conditions even more difficult for photographers.

Stanier '8F' 2-8-0 No 48309 prepares to leave Shepton Mallet with the LCGB 'Wessex Downsman' railtour of 4 April 1965, and head south over the SDJR to Bournemouth West. Towards the end of the line's life '8Fs' were common on the SDJR. 'Modified Hall' No 6963 *Throwley Hall* had brought the train to Bristol from Reading New Junction via Pewsey and Bradford-on-Avon after taking over from 'S15' No 30839, which had hauled the train from Waterloo via Ascot. This tour was so popular that it was repeated a month later (see page 60).

SDJR '7F' 2-8-0 No 53807, piloting '4F' 0-6-0 No 44558, halts at Evercreech Junction for water before heading north to Bath Green Park with the Home Counties Railway Society SDJR railtour of 7 June 1964. As far as is known this was the last BR special hauled by an SDJR '7F' 2-8-0. The locomotives joined the train at Bournemouth Central rather than at the normal terminus for SDJR trains, Bournemouth West. It had been planned to have the last two SDJR '7Fs' in service double-heading the train, namely Nos 53807 and 53809, but evidently the '4F' had to be substituted at a late stage for No 53809. The '4F' was one of the five built specifically for the Somerset & Dorset in April 1922 by Armstrong Whitworth and survived on the line until December 1964.

SCOTTISH PRESERVED LOCOMOTIVES

Above: Caledonian Railway Single No 123 pauses at Stirling for water *en route* to Callander on the CR route to Oban, having started from Glasgow with the first day of the SLS/BLS four-day 'Scottish Rambler' railtour on 12 April 1963. No 123 was designed and built in 1886 by Neilson & Co for that year's Edinburgh International Exhibition. It was destined to be the last 'single-driver' locomotive to operate in Great Britain, and on its withdrawal in 1935 it was preserved by the LMS. After this second operational career, No 123 was retired to the Glasgow Museum of Transport.

Left: One of the four preserved pre-Grouping locomotives returned to traffic by the Scottish Region in the early 1960s, North British 'Glen'-class 4-4-0 No 256 *Glen Douglas* runs into the station of Strathmiglo, on the line from Ladybank to Kinross, with the 1963 'Scottish Rambler' on 13 April 1963, before continuing to Alloa via the Devon Valley line. One of 32 locomotives built to a Reid design between 1913 and 1920, the 'Glens' were traditionally associated with the West Highland line.

Built by Sharp, Stewart & Co in 1894, Highland Railway 'Jones Goods' 4-6-0 No 103, another pre-Grouping locomotive restored by the Scottish Region, has a particular place in Britain's railway history, in that it was the first 4-6-0 locomotive to operate on a British railway. Withdrawn by the LMS in 1934, it was, like No 123, preserved by the company. It was restored to operational condition in 1959, and ran a number of specials including the 'Scottish Rambler' railtours. Having previously traversed the branch from East Kilbride and Linwood, and other goods branches around Glasgow, it is seen here entering Paisley St James with the 1965 'Scottish Rambler' on 17 April 1965, heading for Greenock Princes Pier via the Caledonian route.

HORSHAM–GUILDFORD

On 24 June 1962 the LCGB 'Sussex Coast Limited' railtour pauses at Cranleigh with 'T9' 4-4-0 No 120 on its first outing since its preservation in sage-green LSWR livery. The special was heading from Guildford for Horsham, where two LBSCR tank locomotives would take over. By mid-1961 the number of active 'T9s' was down to three, Nos 30120, 30313 and 30709. All finished work a few weeks later and were withdrawn to Eastleigh. No 30120 was chosen for official preservation, was given a comprehensive overhaul at Eastleigh Works, and emerged in LSWR colours in late March 1962. It was used on certain local turns, such as the Portsmouth portion of the Brighton–Plymouth through working and Basingstoke semi-fasts, as well as on railtours. It was retired from regular use in July 1963, and reappeared, immaculate in BR lined black, on the Mid-Hants Railway in May 1983. It is now active on the Bodmin & Wenford Railway as BR No 30120.

About to visit the freight-only Midhurst branch with the LCGB 'Sussex Coast Limited' railtour of 24 June 1962, an immaculate ex-LBSCR 'E4' 0-6-2T No 32503 and 'E6' 0-6-2T No 32617 take over from preserved 'T9' 4-4-0 No 120 at Horsham. The 'E4' class was the most numerous of R. J. Billinton's 0-6-2T classes, 75 of them being built at Brighton Works between 1897 and 1902. They were largely confined to the Southern Railway's Central Section, and by this date only 10 remained — five at Brighton, four at Nine Elms and one at Eastleigh. One of the class, No 32473, is preserved on the Bluebell Railway in East Sussex.

The RCTS/LCGB 'Midhurst Belle' tour having arrived from Guildford behind 'USA' 0-6-0T No 30064, is backed out of the Guildford-line platform at Christ's Hospital by immaculate 'Q'-class 0-6-0 No 30530. The train is about to head down the Horsham–Arundel main line to Hardnam Junction, from where it will take the freight-only branch to Midhurst before proceeding to Littlehampton. This was the final passenger working over the branch before its closure to all traffic on 10 May 1966.

No 30530 had been fitted with a BR chimney, replacing Bulleid's unsuccessful Lemaître exhaust, in 1953, and by 18 October 1964, when this photograph was taken, was one of seven 'Qs' officially in traffic, although in practice some of these were in store and others retained for winter snowplough duties at Eastleigh, Guildford, Redhill and Salisbury. It would be withdrawn in December 1964, ending its days as shed pilot at Nine Elms.

The unrelenting withdrawal of SR steam locomotives during the mid-1960s meant that the variety of classes was rapidly shrinking, and consequently the small fleet of 'USA' tank engines suddenly found favour with railtour organisers. Here 'USA' 0-6-0T No 30064, in BR lined green and now the shed pilot at Guildford, swings round the curve at Peasmarsh Junction with the RCTS/LCGB 'Midhurst Belle' railtour of 18 October 1964, *en route* to Christ's Hospital and a locomotive change.

Fourteen 'USAs' were acquired in 1946 from the USA Army Transportation Corps, chiefly to replace the ageing ex-LSWR 'B4' 0-4-0Ts working in Southampton Docks. Six of them were painted in lined green during 1963/4, and several survive in preservation on the Bluebell, Kent & East Sussex and Keighley & Worth Valley railways.

Although the 'Q1s' were regarded as the Southern Railway's ugly ducklings, several appeared on railtours in the latter years. By the time of the LCGB 'Wealdsman' tour of 13 June 1965 the class was down to six survivors, which were employed on the various freight and ballast duties. No 33006 had been employed on an REC special over the Horsham–Guildford line the day before, which was the last day of normal operation. (The next day, being Sunday, had no scheduled service.) Having worked some freight and passenger services on the line, Nos 33006 and 33027 were booked to head the last stage of the tour from Horsham to Guildford and then to Waterloo via Cobham. Here they are seen passing the signal box at Slinfold with the 'Wealdsman', which was the very last train over the line.

GWR TANK ENGINES

Right: At Swindon, ex-GWR '14xx' 0-4-2T No 1444 waits to leave with the Great Western Preservation Society's railtour of branch lines on 20 September 1964. The special visited the Calne branch and others. By this time there were few of the '14xx' class left working; the only passenger service left was the Gloucester–Chalford push-pull service.

Below: One of the last operational GWR 0-6-0 pannier tanks in BR service, No 9773, specially cleaned and sporting a Great Western number on the buffer-beam, heads down the Fairford–Witney branch (by now a freight-only line, used only by traffic from the Witney Blanket Co) with the LCGB 'Western Ranger' railtour of 15 August 1965. Having taken over from a '28xx' 2-8-0 at Radley, No 9773 had earlier headed the train down the branch to Abingdon, on which passenger services had ceased with effect from 18 June 1962.

A late survivor of the GWR '61xx' class of 2-6-2Ts, No 6106 (since preserved at Didcot) leaves Kensington Olympia to head up the main line to Southall, where pannier tank No 9773 would take over to run up the freight-only Brentford and Staines West branches, closed to passengers in May 1965. Hauling the LCGB/REC 'Thames Valley' railtour of 27 July 1965, No 6106 would later visit the Henley-on-Thames branch.

NORTH BRITISH RAILWAY LOCOMOTIVES

Right: A rather dirty ex-NBR 'J37' 0-6-0, No 64603, prepares to leave South Queensferry Goods for the junction with the main line at Dalmeny. At the other end of the train is preserved 'D34' 4-4-0 No 256 *Glen Douglas*, the pair having headed down the branch with the SLS/BLS 'Scottish Rambler' from Edinburgh Waverley on 13 April 1963. From Dalmeny the 'Glen' would continue to Thornton Junction, where another 'J37', this time an immaculate No 64618, would take over for a visit to the Leslie branch via the junction at Markinch. The passenger stock had to be fly-shunted back over the viaduct immediately outside the station in order for the 'J37' to run round. The branch served the paper mill at Leslie but had been closed to passengers for 30 years.

Below: At Edinburgh Waverley on 25 June 1966 'J37' 0-6-0s Nos 64570 and 64518 prepare to back down onto the Warwickshire Railway Society 'Aberdonian' railtour and haul the train to Anstruther, then the limit of the coast line to St Andrews, where the locomotives were turned on the old turntable. This tour was the last run from London to Aberdeen and back, via a circuitous route, with steam used all the way, and was also one of the last specials to use 'J37' locomotives.

Built between 1888 and 1900 by the North British Railway, 128 locomotives of the 'J36' class survived to pass into BR ownership, and a few remained in service to the end of steam in Scotland in 1966. Here, one of the last active 'J36s', No 65345, takes water at Musselburgh, the terminus of a short branch off the East Coast main line, having run round Edinburgh (starting at the Corstorphine branch) with the RSS 'J36 Rail Tour' of 31 August 1966. This date marked the end of steam in Scotland apart from one or two 'J36s' retained at Bathgate shed for colliery workings.

THE 'CUCKOO LINE'

Above: A grubby 'U'-class 2-6-0, No 31803, pilots clean 'N'-class 2-6-0 No 31411 up the climb through Rotherfield & Mark Cross station *en route* to Eastbourne with the 'Wealdsman' railtour, the last train to travel over the entire length of the 'Cuckoo Line' before its complete closure on 13 June 1965. All traffic was withdrawn as far as Hailsham, but the line to Polegate stayed open for another three years. The tour had already traversed the Three Bridges–East Grinstead branch and the line through Forest Row to Groombridge Junction behind these locomotives. It marked the effective elimination of steam traction on the Central Section of the Southern Region; the Horsham–Guildford line closed at the same time. The dirty 'U' was an unfortunate last-minute replacement for a clean but failed locomotive.

Left: Ex-LSWR Class M7 0-4-4T No 30055 and preserved 'T9' 4-4-0 No 120 wait in the evening sun at Eastbourne before leaving with the LCGB 'Sussex Coast Limited' railtour of 24 June 1962. They would head the train back to Rotherfield on the 'Cuckoo Line', where the 'M7' would be detached after the climb up through Mayfield, as seen opposite. The 'T9' then proceeded to London Bridge via East Grinstead and Oxted. By this time only 19 of the once-ubiquitous 'M7' class survived.

Right: Looking very smart, 'M7' No 30055 stands at Rotherfield & Mark Cross, having piloted preserved 'T9' No 120 on the LCGB 'Sussex Coast Limited' railtour from Eastbourne.

SOUTHERN ON SHED

Above: With Light Pacific No 34012 *Launceston* in the background, immaculate Class A1X 'Terrier' No 32636 (originally LBSCR No 72 *Fenchurch*) stands on shed at Brighton before heading the RCTS 'Sussex Special' of 7 October 1962 to Seaford and Newhaven with 'E6' 0-6-2T No 32416. The Stroudley 'Terriers' were built at Brighton Works in the early 1870s; 12 of them remained at the time of this photograph, nine with BR and three already preserved. Subsequently *Fenchurch* too passed into preservation and now runs on the Bluebell Railway.

Right: 'E6' No 32418 on shed after arrival at Newhaven Town for servicing, in company with another 'A1X', No 32670, before double-heading No 32636 back to Brighton with the RCTS special. The 'E6' class, 12 in number, were the last of Billinton's radial tank locomotives, and were used for shunting and freight in the London area before being displaced by diesels. None was preserved.

Far right: One of only two unrebuilt Light Pacifics to survive to the end of steam, No 34023 *Blackmore Vale* stands under the coaling stage at Weymouth shed, possibly for the last time, in preparation for the run back to Salisbury with the last RCTS 'Farewell to Steam' special, on 18 June 1967, which it double-headed with rebuilt Light Pacific No 34108 *Wincanton*.

SUSSEX BYWAYS

Above: A pair of ex-LBSCR locomotives, dating from the turn of the century — Class E4 0-6-2T No 32503 and larger Class E6 0-6-2T No 32417 — take water at Midhurst, having run up the branch line with the penultimate passenger working from Hardham Junction, on the Horsham–Littlehampton main line, with the LCGB 'Sussex Coast Limited' railtour of 24 June 1962. By this time Midhurst was the freight-only terminus of a line that formerly ran through to Petersfield (LSWR) on the Portsmouth main line. In those days it had a junction with the former Meon Valley line (LBSCR) down to Chichester, which closed to passengers on 7 July 1935. The line was closed to passenger traffic between Pulborough, Midhurst and Petersfield on 5 February 1955, but was kept open from Pulborough to Midhurst until October 1964. The connection to Petworth lasted until 20 May 1966.

Right: Beautifully groomed 'N'-class Mogul No 31411 prepares to leave Partridge Green on the branch from Horsham to Brighton via Shoreham, heading the RCTS/LCGB 'Sussex Downsman' special of 22 March 1964. It hauled the train back to Three Bridges, where 'Q1' No 33027 took over for the run to Tunbridge Wells West via East Grinstead. At Tunbridge Wells West, Light Pacific No 34066 would take over to traverse the 'Cuckoo line' (see page 7). With the ongoing electrification and 'dieselisation', only 42 'Ns' now remained of the 80 built.

A pause for photographs at Steyning before Bulleid 'Battle of Britain' Pacific No 34050 *Royal Observer Corps* leaves with the returning LCGB 'Wealdsman' railtour up the Shoreham–Horsham line on 13 June 1965. This was one of the last specials over this branch before its closure at the end of the year. The locomotive had come on at Haywards Heath, and took the train onwards via Hove, Shoreham and Steyning to Christ's Hospital, where two 'Q1s' took over for the run to Guildford and Waterloo. Closure to all traffic north of Beeding Cement Works was effected on Monday 7 March 1966, though the line south remained open until May 1980 for cement-works traffic.

CROSS-COUNTRY

Above: Light Pacific No 34038 *Lynton* climbs to the summit of the Didcot, Newbury & Southampton line near Highclere with the RCTS 'East Midlander' railtour of 9 May 1964, *en route* from Didcot to Eastleigh via the GWR station of Winchester Chesil, the only station left open for freight on the line. The tour had started at Nottingham Victoria, hauled by a Stanier Pacific via the Great Central and Banbury as far as Didcot, where the SR locomotive took over. The DNS line was by now a shadow of its former self, passenger services having ceased on 7 March 1960. Latterly its principal traffic consisted of oil trains from Fawley to the Midlands, hauled by BR Standard '9Fs', but these were soon diverted via Basingstoke.

Right: Midland '4F' 0-6-0 No 43953 runs through Shireoaks Midland station, passing the new diesel depot (background, left) with the RCTS 'Midland Locomotive Requiem' tour of 16 October 1965. Bound for the Glapwell Colliery branch, the train would return to Nuneaton Abbey Street by way of Chesterfield, Ambergate and Leicester.

MAUNSELL COMMEMORATIVE

'Q'-class 0-6-0 No 30545, with BR-style chimney, pulls away from Staines Central on 3 January 1965 with the second leg of the LCGB 'Maunsell Commemorative' railtour to Reading, having assisted 'U'-class Mogul No 31639 on the run up the freight-only branch from Wimbledon to Tooting Goods and back via Merton Park. By this time only three 'Qs' — Nos 30535/45/8 — remained in service. Steam working of passenger trains via Merton Abbey to Tooting ceased when the Haydons Road direct line was electrified in 1929.

In the last of the afternoon light 'N'-class 2-6-0 No 31411 immaculately turned out by Redhill shed, speeds away from Redhill on the Tonbridge line with the LCGB 'Maunsell Commemorative' railtour of 3 January 1965, which marked the complete elimination of steam on the Southern's Central Section between Reading, Redhill and Tonbridge, this line had been a final stronghold of the Maunsell Moguls on passenger work. No 31411 headed this final leg of the special back to London Victoria via the Crowhurst spur, the East Grinstead–Oxted line and East Croydon.

'N'-class 2-6-0 No 31831 poses for photographers at North Camp, near Aldershot, on the way to Guildford and Redhill with the third leg of the 'Maunsell Commemorative' railtour of 3 January 1965. By this stage only 12 'Ns' and 10 'Us' were left in service, mainly to assist with the electrification of the SR main line on ballast trains.

Beautifully turned out by Feltham shed, Maunsell 'S15' 4-6-0 No 30837 leaves Alresford for Eastleigh with the LCGB 'S15 Commemorative' railtour of 9 January 1966. The locomotive had been withdrawn in September 1965, and was specially resurrected for this special. The tour was repeated a week later, but on that occasion the weather was snowy, so the train was double-headed with 'U'-class Mogul No 31639 'over the Alps' to Eastleigh (see page 112). Built at Eastleigh in 1928, No 30837 was one of 25 Maunsell 'S15s', and was broken up at Cashmore's, Newport, in September 1966.

SOUTH WESTERN SUBURBAN

Above: Immaculate BR Class 4 2-6-4T No 80145 rounds the curve out of Teddington near Fulwell Junction on a beautiful winter morning with the LCGB's 100th railtour, the 'South Western Suburban', of 5 February 1967, which it headed from Wimbledon Park to Shepperton.

Right: The Shepperton branch was part of the LSWR electrification scheme that started in 1917, so it saw few steam-hauled passenger services thereafter. One exception was the third leg of the LCGB 'South Western Suburban' railtour. Here, rebuilt Light Pacific No 34100 *Appledore* glints in the winter sun as it pulls away from Shepperton heading for Twickenham, having taken over from the Standard tank locomotive seen opposite.

Because they were relatively light and could negotiate the sharp curves, the three surviving Beattie 2-4-0 well tanks of 1874/5 vintage were kept in service, principally for china-clay traffic, on the mineral line between Wadebridge and Wenford Bridge. In August 1962 they were finally withdrawn, and were replaced by ex-GWR '1366' 0-6-0 pannier tanks, but they remained in store at Eastleigh shed. Two of them, Nos 30585 and 30587, were brought up to London to work two RCTS/SLS 'South Western Suburban' railtours from Waterloo to Hampton Court and Shepperton. Here they are seen about to leave Surbiton on the outward run to Hampton Court with the first of these trains, which ran in fine weather on 2 December 1962. Note the stationmaster in grey overcoat and bowler hat, overseeing operations. By the time they reached Hampton Court, the locomotives had run short of water and nearly had to drop their fires, but they were rescued by the local fire brigade. Both of them were preserved and now run in BR black livery on the Bodmin & Wenford Railway and at the Buckinghamshire Railway Centre at Quainton Road.

Right: Here, again on 2 December 1962, the two Beattie well tanks have pulled their stock out of Hampton Court station, run round the train, and are now standing by the signalbox awaiting their return to London.

The second of the two RCTS/SLS railtours, which ran two weeks later, did not have such good weather; on that occasion the two tanks ran back-to-back, which made for less attractive photographs.

Below right: Two of the last workings by a Urie 'H16' 4-6-2T were on the railtours of 2 and 16 December 1962 commemorating the passing of the Beattie well tanks. On both occasions the locomotive in question was No 30517, very well groomed by Feltham shed. Here, on 2 December, it is seen running round at Chessington South, having arrived from Wimbledon goods yard. The 'H16s' spent most of their career working transfer freights across London, handling empty stock at Clapham Junction, and for a short time in 1960/1, working oil trains from Fawley. All were withdrawn by the end of the year, as were the similar Urie 'G16' 4-8-0T hump-shunting locomotives.

'SCOTTISH RAMBLER' 1965

Right: Class A4 Pacific No 60031 *Golden Plover* pauses for water at Galashiels *en route* from Edinburgh to Carlisle over the Waverley route with the 'Scottish Rambler' on 18 April 1965. Later in the day it returned to Glasgow over Beattock Bank in fading light and a shower of snow.

Below: One of the most popular of the quartet of pre-Grouping locomotives preserved by the Scottish Region was Caledonian Railway Single No 123. In Caledonian blue livery and with two Caledonian coaches in tow, it is seen here on 13 April 1965 near Merchiston, between Glasgow Central and Edinburgh Princes Street, with the first part of the Easter SLS/BLS 'Scottish Rambler'.

Preserved Great North of Scotland Railway No 49 *Gordon Highlander* (once BR Class D40 No 62277) pauses at Midcalder *en route* from Glasgow Central to Edinburgh and Leith Central with the first part of the 1965 SLS/BLS 'Scottish Rambler' railtour. The other part of the train was hauled by Caledonian No 123 and its two Caledonian coaches to Edinburgh Princes Street. At its destination each portion was taken over by BR Class 2 2-6-0 for a circular run to Balerno and Slateford and back to Leith and Edinburgh, Nos 78046 and 78054 being the locomotives in question. Nos 49 and 123 finally joined up at Carstairs for the run back to Glasgow on 19 April, the last time either locomotive appeared in use on a special before they retired to the museum in Glasgow. No 49 was one of 21 locomotives of a class designed by William Pickersgill and built between 1898 and 1920. The last eight, of which No 49 was one, had superheaters and extended smokeboxes. The class was progressively withdrawn between 1947 and 1958. *Gordon Highlander* was the last to be withdrawn. In preservation it was restored to its pre-Grouping livery by the Scottish Region.

ISLE OF WIGHT

Right: By the end of 1962 the only 'O2'-class 0-4-4T locomotives remaining in service were those on the Isle of Wight. Here No W14 *Fishbourne* stands in the centre road at Ryde Pier Head station, ready to depart with the LCGB 'Vectis' railtour of 4 October 1964, having joined forces with No W28 *Ashey* to visit both of the remaining lines on the island. The tour was first taken from Waterloo to Guildford behind 'Q1' 0-6-0 No 33026. At Guildford BR Class 7MT Pacific No 70000 *Britannia* took over for the remainder of the journey to Portsmouth Harbour via Reading and Eastleigh.

Far right: A year later Class O2s Nos W24 *Calbourne* and W14 *Fishbourne* pause for a photo-stop at Wroxall on the climb from Shanklin to Ventnor while double-heading the somewhat premature LCGB 'Vectis Farewell' railtour of 3 October 1965. The train later headed for Cowes, but reached only as far as Newport owing to the failure of one of the locomotives. *Calbourne* was the last 'O2' to go through Ryde Works, hence the lack of lining in its livery, and it would be the only one to survive into preservation, on what is now the Isle of Wight Steam Railway and at the time of writing has been outshopped in BR black lined livery once more.

AGAINST THE GRADE

The widespread introduction of BRCW Type 3 diesel locomotives, coupled with a decline in freight traffic, rendered many Class S15 4-6-0s redundant, and the final members of the class — Nos 30824/37-9/42 — were withdrawn from Feltham shed in September 1965. No 30837, however, was specially retained for a commemorative railtour. Here, polished to perfection by shed staff, it makes a memorable sight as it storms the 1-in-80 climb to Medstead from Alton on its way 'over the Alps' to Eastleigh with the first of the LCGB's 'S15 Commemorative' railtours, on 9 January 1966. The tour was so popular that a repeat was arranged for the following Sunday, but that ran in very different weather (see page 112).

One of the last operational '8F' 2-8-0s, No 48773, breasts the 1-in-68 climb southbound to Copy Pit Summit, near Clivinger, in the evening light on the last leg (from Rose Grove to Manchester Victoria) of the SVRS/MRTS 'Farewell to Steam' special of 28 July 1968. This locomotive was also the '8F' used on the last LCGB farewell special on 4 August 1968, the day after the end of normal BR steam operation; it was subsequently preserved and returned to working order on the Severn Valley Railway.

SOUTH MIDLANDS

Right: A smart '4F' 0-6-0, No 44414, waits to leave the terminus of the freight-only branch at Newport Pagnell with the South Bedfordshire Locomotive Club 'Cobbler' railtour of 19 September 1964, having run there from Luton Bute Street via Dunstable and Leighton Buzzard on the main line. Note the locomotive inspector looking after the children viewing the locomotive; his suit, tie and bowler hat betoken his pride in the job. The branch had been closed to passengers as recently as 7 September 1964, and was steam-operated to the last. After Newport Pagnell the special headed via Blisworth and Northampton (Bridge Street) to Wellingborough, where a second '4F' took over for a run up the short branch to Higham Ferrers.

Far right: Stanier 'Black Five' No 45292, of Willesden shed, prepares to leave Bedford Midland Road with the LCGB 'South Midlands' railtour of 17 October 1964 before running down the by now truncated section of the LNWR Cambridge–Oxford line to Swanbourne.

HAYLING ISLAND FAREWELL

Last rites on the Hayling Island branch. Although 2 November 1963 was the final day of timetabled services — there being no Sunday service — the very last train down the branch was an LCGB 'Hayling Farewell' railtour the following day. Resplendent in the sunshine, 'A1X' 0-6-0T No 32636 approaches Langstone Halt, banked at the rear by another 'A1X', No 32670. These two 'Terriers', built in 1872, were the first of their class to be built.

Above: Class A1X No 32670 backs up the farewell train seen opposite, heading for the timber bridge over to Hayling Island itself. It was owing to the weight restriction on this bridge that the last 'Terriers' remaining in BR service worked on this branch, having in the past carried thousands of holidaymakers.

Left: No 32670 waits in the low evening light before leaving Hayling Island station with the returning LCGB 'Hayling Farewell' special of 3 November 1963.

NORTH WALES

Above: After electric haulage from Euston to Crewe, 'Britannia' Pacific No 70004 *William Shakespeare* hauled the LCGB 'Conway Valley' railtour of 24 September 1966 along the North Wales Coast line to Llandudno Junction. There a pair of Stanier 2-6-4 tanks, Nos 42574 and 42644, took over for the run up the Conway Valley branch via Bettws-y-Coed. In this photograph the Staniers arrive at Blaenau Festiniog (as it was then spelt) under towering mountains of slate.

Right: Later in the day the 'Britannia' rejoined the train at Llandudno and took it on to Rhyl, where the last operational 'Crab' 2-6-0, No 42942, took over, being seen pausing at Rhuddlan on the way down the branch (by now freight-only) to Denbigh, which once provided a connection to Corwen on the line from Ruabon to Barmouth from Llandudno Junction. Only one more special with this 'Crab' occurred after this date. Note the damaged cylinder cover.

'SCOTTISH RAMBLER' 1963

Left: The SLS/BLS 'Scottish Rambler' railtour of 1963 was run over four days, 12-15 April. Here preserved ex-North British 'D34' 4-4-0 No 256 *Glen Douglas* pauses for water at Dunfermline Upper while heading from Edinburgh to Ladybank and the Devon Valley line to Alloa via Kinross on 13 April, the second day of the tour.

Below: From Alloa ex-North British 'J36' 0-6-0 No 65323 was used for a run down the freight-only branch to Alva, close to the Ochil Hills. The locomotive is seen having run round its train prior to returning to Alloa, where it would hand back to *Glen Douglas* for the return to Edinburgh Waverley.

Right: *Glen Douglas* prepares to leave Rumbling Bridge after a photo-stop, while traversing the Devon Valley line from Kinross to Alloa on 13 April.

Having run round its train at Duns, ex-LNER 'B1' 4-6-0 No 61324 awaits departure back up the branch to Reston on the Berwick–Edinburgh main line on 14 April 1963. The Reston branch was originally a through line connecting with the Waverley route at St Boswells, but it was severed by the 1948 floods and was thereafter worked only as separate branches from each end. The 'B1', from Edinburgh St Margarets shed, later hauled the train from Tweedmouth through Coldstream and then continued to St Boswells for a return trip up the other end of the truncated line to Greenlaw.

Left: No 61324 halts at Coldstream to allow an LMS 2-6-0 (just visible at the rear of the train) to head the train down the freight-only branch to Wooler, by this time the terminus of a line that had once run through to Alnwick. Later the 'B1' continued to St Boswells and up the other section of the truncated branch to Greenlaw and back. From St Boswells the train continued to Hawick, where 'A3' Pacific No 60041 *Salmon Trout* took over for a run to Carlisle via the Waverley route.

Below: On 15 April 1963 ex-Caledonian Railway Drummond 'Standard Goods' 0-6-0 No 57375 backs on to its train of goods wagons at Millisle to convey the 'Scottish Rambler' passengers down the short branch to Garlieston on the Portpatrick & Wigtown Joint line from Newton Stewart to Whithorn. The 'Standard Goods', colloquially known as the 'Jumbos', were introduced in 1883 and ultimately became the CR's most numerous class.

SOUTH COAST

Above: Immaculate LBSCR locomotives 'A1X' No 32636 and 'E6' No 32418 run round at Seaford branch terminus to return the RCTS 'Sussex Special' railtour to Newhaven Harbour. They went on shed at Newhaven, in company with 'A1X' No 32670 and 'E4' No 32503, before returning to Brighton via Lewes on 7 October 1962. Having been brought from London Bridge to Brighton by 'Schools' 4-4-0 No 30925 *Cheltenham*, the special returned to London via Shoreham and Horsham behind 'K'-class Mogul No 32353, this being the last occasion on which a 'K'-class locomotive was used on a railtour.

Right: Double-chimneyed BR Class 4 No 75070 enters Fareham station with the RCTS 'Solent Limited' railtour of 20 March 1966, having brought the special from Southampton Ocean Terminal after it had made a trip down the Fawley branch with two 'USA' tanks (see page 11).

A well-cleaned 'Q1' 0-6-0, No 33020, with No 33006 of the same class banking at the rear, pulls energetically up the grade from the closed station of Lavant with the LCGB 'Vectis Farewell' railtour of 3 October 1965. Starting from Waterloo, the train had travelled to Chichester via the Portsmouth line behind 'West Country' Pacific No 34002 *Salisbury*, which would now take over for the run to Portsmouth Harbour and a connection with the Isle of Wight, where the railtour continued (see page 45). At one time the Lavant branch continued north to a junction at Midhurst but was closed to passengers in 1935 (and partly to freight in 1951) and was truncated at Lavant in 1953. Final closure did not take effect until March 1991.

GREAT WESTERN LOCOMOTIVES

Right: Having been brought from Paddington by well-turned-out 'Grange' 4-6-0 No 6841 *Marlas Grange*, the RCTS Gloucestershire railtour of 21 July 1963 arrives at Avonmouth Docks, where one of the Port of Bristol Authority's 0-6-0 Peckett tank locomotives would take over for a tour of the PBA railway network. The PBA shed was the home of 10 steam locomotives — seven Pecketts and three Avonsides — as well as a number of diesels. The tour subsequently visited the Sharpness, Nailsworth, Dursley and Stroud (LMS) branches behind BR Class 3 2-6-2T No 82036, but because a long restaurant car got stuck while being shunted at one of the branch exits from the main line the tour ran hours late, and many participants (including your author) abandoned the tour at Stroud and caught a normal service train back to Paddington.

Below: Having taken over from an 'S15' at Reading New Junction, 'Modified Hall' 4-6-0 No 6963 *Throwley Hall*, by now minus nameplates and front number plate, draws into Devizes station on 2 May 1965 with the second LCGB 'Wessex Downsman' railtour, bound for Bristol via Bradford-on-Avon.

Having negotiated the east curve off the main line at Foxhall Junction after a works visit to Swindon Works, the last operational 'County' Class 4-6-0, No 1011 *County of Chester*, accelerates away from Didcot North Junction, heading back to Birmingham with the SLS 'County Farewell' special of 20 September 1964. This was indeed the last outing of any of the 'Counties', none of which was preserved.

HAMPSHIRE BRANCH LINES (2)

Above: 'Battle of Britain' Pacific No 34057 *Biggin Hill*, now without nameplate or crest, leaves Romsey at the head of the LCGB 'Hampshire Branch Lines' railtour, which it hauled to Southampton on 9 April 1967. By this date *Biggin Hill* was one of only three unrebuilt Bulleid Light Pacifics still in active service.

Right: Later in the day 'USA'-class 0-6-0s Nos 30069 and 30064 enter Fawley station, having run down the branch from Southampton with the LCGB 'Hampshire Branch Lines' railtour. They returned the train up the branch to Totton, where Standard Class 4 2-6-4T No 80151, assisted by 2-6-2T No 41320, took over for the trip to Lymington Pier. The Fawley branch was freight-only by this time, kept in operation only to serve the Esso oil refinery.

BIRKENHEAD FAREWELL (1)

Above: By now preserved, 'Castle' 4-6-0 No 7029 *Clun Castle* comes off its train at Chester station after working the LCGB 'Severn and Dee' special from Wolverhampton High Level on 26 February 1967. The tour had been arranged as the club's farewell to the GWR Paddington–Birkenhead service, and began with electric haulage from London to Nuneaton, where a 'Black Five' took over for the run to Wolverhampton. The special headed back to Crewe behind a rebuilt Crosti '9F', from where it would return to London behind electric traction.

Right: 'Black Five' 4-6-0 No 44680 races up the 1-in-83 bank past Llangollen Junction with the second of two SLS specials from Birmingham to Birkenhead on 5 March 1967, the day after the Ian Allan specials run to mark the end of the service to/from Paddington. The first of the SLS specials was headed by *Clun Castle*.

Above: Returning from Chester to Birmingham late on the afternoon of 4 March 1967, No 7029 *Clun Castle* speeds southwards through Rossett, at the foot of Gresford Bank, with the 'Zulu' — the second of the Ian Allan specials run to commemorate the GWR route between Paddington and Birkenhead.

Right: *Clun Castle* speeds away from Rossett to attack the formidable 3½ mile climb at 1-in-82 of Gresford Bank in fading evening light on 4 March 1967.

SOUTH COAST TERMINI

Left: The last active LBSCR 'K'-class 2-6-0, No 32353, takes water at Bognor Regis, having narrowly avoided being derailed on the turntable in the background, which had had to be hand-turned with the help of passengers. It had hauled the LCGB 'Sussex Coast Limited' from Pulborough on 24 June 1962, and would continue to Haywards Heath, where 'T9' No 120 took over again for the run to Eastbourne (see page 18). The 'K' was an L. B. Billinton design dating from 1913, intended mainly for express freight duties. The class was always based on the Central Section of the Southern, in later years based in roughly equal numbers at Brighton and Three Bridges. They were condemned *en masse* at the end of 1962, even though three of them, including No 32353 (the last of the class, built in 1921), had been in service for only two years since a major overhaul. This example of the LBSCR's final design of tender engine was offered to the Bluebell Railway, but regrettably a lack of funds precluded its purchase.

Left: An unusual visitor to the terminus station of Littlehampton, 'Merchant Navy' Pacific No 35007 *Aberdeen Commonwealth* backs down on to the LCGB/RCTS 'Midhurst Belle' railtour (seen earlier on page 19), taking over from 'Q' 0-6-0 No 30530 to haul the train to Brighton and then Victoria after a visit to the Kemp Town branch (again courtesy of No 30530, which followed the train light-engine from Littlehampton) on 18 October 1964.

Right: Nicely cleaned unrebuilt 'Battle of Britain' 4-6-2 No 34051 *Winston Churchill* waits to leave Bournemouth West with the returning LCGB 'Wessex Downsman' for the return run to London on 4 April 1965. Used to haul Sir Winston's funeral train on 30 January that year, it was subsequently preserved by BR but has yet to be restored to working order.

LMS LOCOMOTIVES

In immaculate condition, one of the last surviving LMS '2P' 4-4-0s, No 40646 (based at Bescot), stands at Luton Bute Street on 14 April 1962, waiting to take over from preserved ex-GNR 'J52' saddle tank No 1247 on the SLS 'Seven Branch Lines' special. The '2P' would head the train back to Birmingham via Dunstable and on to the LMS main line. It had earlier hauled the train from Birmingham to Northampton and over the Midland line to Bedford, double-heading with '2MT' 2-6-2T No 40026 (by now the last of its class), which then continued alone to Hitchin, where the preserved 'J52' was waiting to take the train to Luton via Hertford, Hatfield and Welwyn Garden City.

Above: One of the last operational '4F' 0-6-0s was brought all the way from Workington to Nuneaton Abbey Street to haul the RCTS 'Midland Locomotives Requiem' railtour of 16 October 1965. No 43953 is seen here, immaculately turned out, approaching Egginton Junction as it heads for Mansfield Town via Trent and Nottingham. Although by now one of the last survivors of its class, No 43953 had been among the first to be built to this 1911 Fowler design for the Midland Railway.

Right: The last known Midland '3F' 0-6-0 to operate a special was No 43658, here seen pulling away from Castle Donnington *en route* from Burton-upon-Trent to Derby Midland via Trent with the LCGB 'Midland Limited' railtour on 14 October 1962. The class dated from 1885, and by the time of this special there were only 20 left working. This tour had left Marylebone behind 'B16' 4-6-0 No 61418 (see page 104) and travelled via the Great Central route to Nottingham Victoria, where a 'J11' 0-6-0 tank took over for the second leg as far as Burton; it was also notable for being the last railtour to use an unrebuilt 'Patriot' 4-6-0, No 45543 *Home Guard*, which was in charge for the return journey from Derby to St Pancras, although by then it was too dark for a colour photograph.

DORSET

Right: The former LSWR line from Broadstone Junction to Brockenhurst via Wimborne closed on 16 October 1964, and Wimborne and Ringwood only remained open to freight, the double track between them now worked as a single-line siding. Here we see BR Standard Class 3MT 2-6-0 No 77014 in charge of the LCGB 'Dorset and Hants' railtour on 16 October 1966, as it prepares to leave Ringwood station *en route* to the truncated southerly remains of the S&D line at Blandford Forum via Broadstone Junction. In view of all the reversals required, the '3MT' was assisted on this section by BR Class 4 2-6-0 No 76026 at the other end of the train. No 77014 had come south from the North East in March 1966 to work a railtour and never gone back; it was the only locomotive of this class ever to be shedded on the Southern, and by this time was serving as the last Guildford shed pilot.

Below: The MRTS 'Hants and Dorset Branch Flyer' special of 25 March 1967 was handled by Ivatt 2-6-2T No 41320. Here the Ivatt halts at a manually controlled level crossing, beside an original SDJR sign, as it returns from Blandford Forum to Poole, there to lead the train away down the Swanage branch.

One of the last active unrebuilt Light Pacifics, No 34023 *Blackmore Vale*, pulls away from Corfe Castle, on the branch from Wareham to Swanage, with the LCGB 'Dorset Coast Express' of 7 May 1967. The train twice ran up and down the branch with Standard Class 4 No 76026 at the other end and marked the LCGB's farewell to steam on the Southern Region. By this time only three unmodified and 29 rebuilt Light Pacifics survived, none of them destined to last very much longer.

ISLE OF WIGHT FAREWELL

Above: On 31 December 1966, the last day of BR steam on the Isle of Wight, 'O2' 0-4-4T No W14 *Fishbourne* appeared in public suitably adorned with a small headboard and wreath. Here it pulls off its normal service train after arrival at Shanklin, by then the terminus of the last remaining line open from Ryde Pier Head. By this date the rundown had left most of the class in a grubby state. At the end of operation 10 locomotives were nominally left in service.

Right: The last-day special organised by the LCGB to mark the end of steam on the Isle of Wight waits in the late-afternoon sun to leave Shanklin for the run back to Ryde behind 'O2s' Nos W24 *Calbourne* and W31 *Chale* on 31 December 1966.

SMJ TOURS

Right: The MGNJRS 'Wandering 1500' railtour of 5 October 1963 was operated by ex-LNER 'B12/3'-class 4-6-0 No 61572. The outward route was from Broad Street to Northampton via Olney, and then over the Stratford-upon-Avon & Midland Junction Railway to Stratford-on-Avon Old Town via Blisworth and Towcester the return to London being via Leamington and the West Coast main line. Here No 61572 takes water at Northampton Castle. It was already in private hands, having been saved by the shedmaster at Norwich. This occasion was its only special run before a long period of storage and then restoration. No 61572 finally emerged in working order on the North Norfolk Railway, resplendent in BR lined black, and is the only operational inside-cylinder 4-6-0 left in Britain.

Right: On 12 October 1963 ex-GWR '43xx' 2-6-0 No 6368 and '2251' 0-6-0 No 2246 double-headed the LCGB's 'Thames, Avon & Severn' tour from Woodford Halse to Worcester Shrub Hill via the ex-Stratford-upon-Avon & Midland Joint line, being seen here pausing for photographs at the closed station of Stratford-on-Avon Old Town. By now freight-only, the line would close to all traffic in 1965. The tour had originated from Waterloo, being hauled to Woodford Halse via Reading and Banbury by preserved 'T9' 4-4-0 No 120 and Class U Mogul No 31791.

Southern Railway Class U Mogul No 31639 pilots 'Q1' 0-6-0 No 33006 up the bank from Stratford-upon-Avon to Wilmcote in wintry weather on 7 March 1965, having travelled the SMJR joint line from Fenny Compton to Stratford Old Town with the HCRS 'Six Counties' special. After reversing onto the LMS lines at Leamington Spa the train would continue via Rugby and Northampton to Wellingborough, where both locomotives were serviced before heading the train back to Paddington via Bedford, Oxford and Thame.

MIDLAND MAIN LINE

On 6 June 1964 well-groomed 'Jubilee' 4-6-0 No 45721 *Impregnable* waits to leave St Pancras with the LCGB 'North Countryman' railtour. It would head the train as far as Whitehall Junction, Leeds, where Class V2 2-6-2 No 60923 would take over for the run to Carlisle.

In appalling weather Class V2 2-6-2 No 60923 pauses for water at Skipton on its way back to Leeds City with the LCGB 'North Countryman' tour of 6 June 1964. It had headed the train from Leeds to Carlisle via Ais Gill, and returned via Shap and the line through Ingleton and Clapham with only a short pause for water outside Carlisle Upperby shed. In the gathering gloom, 'A3' Pacific No 60051 *Blink Bonny* returned the train to King's Cross via Doncaster and the East Coast main line. The 'Little North Western' route between Low Gill and Clapham, although still available as a main-line diversionary route at this time, had lost its sparse passenger service as early as 1 February 1954.

DOUBLE-HEADING PACIFICS

Rebuilt Bulleid Light Pacifics Nos 34108 *Wincanton* and 34089 *602 Squadron*, clean but with no plates to identify them, speed along near New Milton with the second leg, from Fareham to Wareham, of the last 'Farewell to Southern Steam' railtour, run by the RCTS on 18 June 1967.

At Wareham No 34089 was joined by Standard 2-6-4 tank No 80146 for a run down the branch to Swanage and back before taking the train on to Weymouth unaided.

After a photo-stop outside the already-closed station (see page 1), Light Pacifics Nos 34102 *Lapford* and 34057 *Biggin Hill* run through Grateley with the LCGB 'Bridport Belle' railtour of 22 January 1967. At Westbury, rebuilt Light Pacific No 34013 took over, taking the ex-GWR route as far as Maiden Newton for a visit to the Bridport branch behind two Ivatt 2-6-2Ts (Nos 41320 and 41295), only eight of which now remained in service. Unfortunately the wet weather rendered the tank locomotives unable to climb the steep bank from Powerstock on the return from Bridport, and after several failed attempts they stalled at the bottom of the bank, having to be rescued by a diesel locomotive. By now the tour was running several hours late, and 'Merchant Navy' No 35030 waited in vain at Maiden Newton to return the train to London.

SCARBOROUGH–WHITBY

Above: The first of two views featuring well-turned-out ex-LNER 'B1' 4-6-0 No 61031 *Reedbuck* in charge of the RCTS 'North Eastern Limited' tour on 2 May 1964. Here the locomotive has slipped to a stand on wet rails during the steep climb from Flying Hall to Ravenscar on the coast between Scarborough and Whitby. It had to set back several times, with much sanding of the rails by the fireman, before the bank was finally surmounted. The special, which originated from Newcastle, had been headed by an 'A3' Pacific as far as York, where the 'B1' took over for the journey to Scarborough via Market Weighton and Bridlington.

Right: Having reached Whitby, which involved reversing down from the high-level West Cliff station (the coast line being already closed beyond this point), the 'B1' shunts the sidings outside the station, with the ruined Whitby Abbey visible across the river on the skyline. From Whitby the train would continue via Battersby Junction to Middlesbrough, where the last ex-NER 'Q7' 0-8-0, No 64367 (already earmarked for preservation), would take over for the final leg to Newcastle via Wellfield Junction and Sunderland.

THE GOSPORT BRANCH

Above: Well-kept 'U'-class Mogul No 31639 was used on many of the last Southern Region specials, together with 'N'-class No 31411. By this time only three 'Us' — Nos 31639, 31791 and 31803, all based at Guildford — were left in service, and even they had survived only to help with electrification of the ex-LSWR main line to Bournemouth. Here No 31639 is seen leaving Fareham for a short trip down the Gosport branch as part of the RCTS 'Solent Limited' railtour of 20 March 1966. After returning tender-first up the branch it would double-head the special back to London with BR Standard Class 4 4-6-0 No 75070.

Right: Nicely cleaned 'N'-class 2-6-0 No 31411 departs from under the overall roof of the now disused Gosport station to head up the freight-only branch to Fareham with the SCTS 'Southdown Venturer' tour of 20 February 1966. The Mogul would then haul the train to Portsmouth Harbour, where 'West Country' Pacific No 34013 *Okehampton*, which had been in charge of the outward journey from Victoria via Crowborough, Lewes and Brighton, would take over for the return leg via Guildford to London Bridge.

SOUTHWEST SCOTLAND

Having arrived at Castle Douglas from Carlisle on 15 April 1963, the last day of the 1963 SLS/BLS 'Scottish Rambler' tour, 'Jubilee' 4-6-0 No 45588 *Kashmir* has pulled off the train, to be replaced by Standard Class 4 2-6-4T No 80023 for a run down the branch to Kirkcudbright and back. Apart from trips down the branch lines *en route* using the Standard tank and the Caledonian 'Jumbo' (see page 89) the 'Jubilee' headed the train from Carlisle to Stranraer throughout, via Lockerbie and Dumfries.

On the same day preserved Highland Railway 'Jones Goods' 4-6-0 No 103 and GNSR 4-4-0 No 49 *Gordon Highlander* (BR No 62277) prepare to come off shed at Stranraer to head the 1963 'Scottish Rambler' back over the moors to Glasgow via Barhill and Ayr. The last of its class (designated 'D40' by the LNER and British Railways) to remain operational, *Gordon Highlander* had been withdrawn in 1956 but was restored to working order in the early 1960s. It has since been placed in the Glasgow Museum of Transport.

Left: On 15 April 1963 No 45588 *Kashmir* pauses for water at the isolated Loch Skerrow platform while traversing the former Portpatrick & Wigtownshire Joint line to Stranraer from Carlisle with the 'Scottish Rambler'. This passing platform, remote in the moors of Kirkcudbrightshire, was several miles from the nearest road.

Above: Another leg of the 1963 'Scottish Rambler', seen again on 15 April, was operated by ex-Caledonian Drummond '2F' 0-6-0 No 57375, built in 1894 to an 1883 design. Here it is making heavy smoke after arrival at the overgrown terminus of Garlieston on the short branch from the junction at Millisle. Because the branch was by now freight-only with weight restrictions, the passengers of the SLS/BLS 'Scottish Rambler' had to be conveyed in open wagons from Millisle. The 0-6-0 had earlier headed the special down the Whithorn Peninsula on the former Portpatrick & Wigtownshire Joint line from Newton Stewart to Whithorn.

SOMERSET & DORSET FAREWELL

Above: After taking water, Class 8F 2-8-0 No 48706 departs from Evercreech Junction in a southerly direction with the Great Western Society special of 5 March 1966, the last day of normal operation on the SDJR before complete closure of the line north of Blandford Forum two days later.

Right: Ready to take over from a pair of Ivatt tanks which had headed the train from Templecombe and up the branch to Highbridge, immaculate unrebuilt Light Pacifics Nos 34006 *Bude* and 34057 *Biggin Hill* wait in the pilot road at Evercreech Junction to haul the LCGB 'Farewell to the SDJR' to Bath before returning to Bournemouth on 5 March 1966, the last day of normal operation on the Somerset & Dorset line. From Bournemouth the train was returned to Waterloo by 'Merchant Navy' Pacific No 35028 *Clan Line*, which had earlier powered the outward leg to Templecombe.

NORTH EASTERN FAREWELL

An immaculate No 62005, one of the last active 'K1' 2-6-0s, from Heaton shed, Newcastle, pulls away from Redmire, piloting a BR Type 2 (Class 25) diesel with the SLS 'Three Dales' tour of 20 May 1967. Redmire was the limit of the truncated Wensleydale branch from Northallerton, which formerly ran through to Hawes and Garsdale. The passenger service to Hawes had been withdrawn on 26 April 1964, but the branch remained open as far as Redmire to serve the limestone works seen (with Bolton Castle beyond) behind the train. This SLS special was the last steam-hauled enthusiast special in this part of the North East, and was the last steam train to traverse this branch in BR days; but 40 years later, the same 'K1', preserved and restored to working order by the NELPG, worked a repeat 'Three Dales' train over the line, this time with diesel assistance at the rear.

The 'Three Dales' tour also visited the branches to Catterick Camp, Weardale and Richmond. Here the 'K1' prepares to leave the attractive terminus at Richmond before heading for the Weardale branch, which like the Hawes branch had been kept open to serve the cement works at Eastgate, but had closed to passengers as early as 29 June 1953. Fortunately part of both these attractive branches are now being operated as preserved railways, but steam operation on the Richmond and Catterick branches (latterley for freight only) ceased at the end of December 1965 with the closure of Darlington steam shed, and was followed by complete line closure in March 1969 with the withdrawal of DMU passenger services.

One of the last of five active 'Jubilees' retained at Leeds Holbeck shed for operation over the Leeds–Carlisle line was No 45562 *Alberta*, withdrawn in September 1967. Here, still at work, it slows for signals at Winning North Junction, having just crossed the viaduct over the Wansbeck River after leaving Ashington, Northumberland, with the returning SLS/Manchester Locomotive Society 'Ashington Rail Tour' of 11 June 1967.

The 'Jubilee' had headed the 'Ashington Rail Tour' from Manchester Exchange to the colliery railway at Ashington. The Ashington Coal Co's system served various collieries; so extensive was it that it operated a 24-hour passenger service of as many as 94 trains a day from Monday to Friday for the miners, but the service had been replaced by buses in 1966. On 11 June 1967 the railtour passengers transferred to three old suburban coaches — two North Eastern Railway elliptical-roof non-corridors and a Furness Railway non-corridor — and travelled the circuit behind NCB 0-6-0T No 39, which was built by Robert Stephenson & Hawthorn in 1954 and scrapped in 1969.

LONGMOOR SPECIALS

Right: 'U'-class Mogul No 31639 arrives at the closed station of Bordon, having headed down the branch from Bentley with the first LCGB 'S15 Commemorative' railtour of 9 January 1966. Although closed to ordinary passengers from 16 September 1957, this branch still gave access to the northern part of the Longmoor Military Railway.

Far right: In 1966 the RCTS ran two railtours to the Longmoor Military Railway. On the second occasion, on 30 April, War Department 2-10-0 *Gordon* made a rare appearance on BR lines, for which special permission had to be obtained. Here it is leaving Woking on the Portsmouth line, heading for the LMR junction at Liss. *Gordon* is now preserved on the Severn Valley Railway.

Below: On the outward run with the second of the RCTS 'Longmoor' specials, *Gordon* climbs the 1-in-130 grade to the summit of the Portsmouth line near Haslemere.

After the second RCTS Longmoor Military Railway special arrived at Liss, the passengers transferred to a train of old coaches and vans, and were taken around the large military circuit by a 'Austerity' 0-6-0ST No 196, here seen leaving the military station. Headed once more by 'WD' 2-10-0 *Gordon*, the special later returned via the main line to Staines, where Standard Class 5 No 73114 took over.

A pair of SR Moguls — 'U'-class No 31791 (rebuilt from a 'River' 2-6-4 tank) and 'N'-class No 31639 — stand at the terminus of Windsor & Eton Riverside in the last of the evening light, with Windsor Castle prominent on the skyline, waiting to take over the second RCTS 'Longmoor' tour of 30 April 1966. This was the last appearance of SR Moguls on a steam railtour before their complete demise. The last Maunsell Moguls in traffic, all allocated to Guildford shed, were Nos 31405, 31408, 31639 and 31791, and were officially withdrawn during June 1966, so this celebrated design missed its 50th birthday.

BIRKENHEAD FAREWELL (2)

Above: Castle' No 4079 *Pendennis Castle* backs down at Chester (LNWR) shed after arriving from Birmingham with the 'Birkenhead Flyer', the first of two Ian Allan specials run on 4 March 1967 to mark the end of the WR service to/from Paddington.

Right: Immaculately restored 'Castle' No 7029 *Clun Castle* basks in the late-afternoon sun at Chester (LNWR) shed before returning to London with the 'Zulu', the second of the Ian Allan specials run on 4 March 1967.

A respectably clean BR '9F' 2-10-0, No 92203, pauses at Hooton station with the second of two SLS specials run on the Birkenhead route on 5 March 1967. The '9F' is hauling the train to Chester from Birkenhead and back, where 'Castle' No 7029 *Clun Castle* will take over for the run back to Birmingham. After its withdrawal in November 1967 No 92203 achieved fame when it was bought by the artist David Shepherd, who preserved it initially on the Longmoor Military Railway.

Cleaner still, another '9F', No 92234, headed the first SLS special from Birkenhead to Chester and back. It is seen here departing after the photo-stop at Hooton. The train was later hauled back to Birmingham by 'Black Five' No 44680 (see page 65). This is was the last time that '9Fs' worked on a special railtour and marked the end of their use in the Birkenhead area.

GREAT CENTRAL

Left: Class B16/2 4-6-0 No 61438 pauses for photographs at Loughborough Central on a misty 14 October 1962 with the LCGB 'Midland Limited' railtour, which it hauled from Marylebone to Nottingham Victoria, where an ex-GER 'J11' 0-6-0 took over for the next leg to Burton-upon-Trent. The 'B16' was a rare visitor to the south of the country.

Right: 'Merchant Navy' Pacific No 35030 *Elder Dempster Lines* prepares to leave Waterloo with the LCGB's 'Great Central' farewell railtour of 3 September 1966. The locomotive gained the Great Central main line via Neasden and after a water stop at Aylesbury ran through to Nottingham Victoria. On the following day the Great Central line between Calvert and Rugby was closed to all traffic, so ending through running from London to the North on the last main line to be built in Britain.

Below: After the arrival of the LCGB 'Great Central Farewell' railtour at Nottingham Victoria, two 'B1' 4-6-0s from Wakefield shed, Nos 61131 and 61173, double-headed the train as far as Elsecar Junction and the electrified Penistone line. Here No 61131 runs round to join the train, having taken water and used the turntable.

OLIVER CROMWELL

Above: On 20 April 1968 the last active 'Britannia', No 70013 *Oliver Cromwell*, beautifully turned out and still with nameplates, waits to leave Fleetwood with the second RCTS 'Lancastrian' railtour, the train having arrived from Liverpool behind immaculate 'Black Five' No 45156 *Ayrshire Yeomanry*. The special later visited Morecambe and Heysham before returning via Hellifield.

Right: No 70013 *Oliver Cromwell*, storms up the 1-in-101 grade past Hogton *en route* from Manchester and Preston to Carnforth via Blackburn and Hellifield with the first steam-hauled leg of the MRTS/SVRS 'Farewell to Steam' tour of 28 July 1968 (see page 47). The train had been diesel-hauled from Birmingham New Street to Stockport, where No 70013 took over.

ENGINE CHANGE

Now preserved and resplendent in LSWR sage-green livery, the last surviving 'T9' 4-4-0, No 120 (latterly BR No 30120), has run forward off its train at Andover Junction to change places with a less-elegant 'Q1' 0-6-0 (No 33038, seen in the distance), which took over the Southern Counties Touring Society's 'Hampshire Venturer' railtour of 10 March 1963 to visit the Bulford Camp military branch and thence to Salisbury. The 'T9' then resumed charge for the run from Salisbury via Romsey to Southampton Docks.

'Black Five' No 45292 arrives at Swanbourne from Bedford Midland Road with the LCGB 'South Midlands Rail Tour' of 17 October 1964, while immaculate 2-6-4T No 42105 waits in the other road to take over the train for the run via Bletchley to Wolverton and then traverse the freight-only Newport Pagnell branch. The 'Black Five' then took the train on to Market Harborough. Passenger traffic had ceased on the latter branch as recently as 7 September 1964, still with steam haulage.

SALISBURY AND BEYOND

Above: 'M7' 0-4-4Ts Nos 30025 and 30026 of Exmouth Junction shed pause at Budleigh Salterton for a photo-stop *en route* to Exmouth with the SCTS 'South Western Limited' railtour of 2 September 1962, having joined the train at Sidmouth Junction. The special had been brought down the main line by the last operational 'Lord Nelson' 4-6-0, No 30861 *Lord Anson*.

Right: Taking water at Seaton, BR Standard Class 4 2-6-4T No 80041 has just traversed the branch from Seaton Junction with the LCGB 'East Devon' railtour of 28 February 1965. The special also visited the branches to Sidmouth and Exmouth using Ivatt 2-6-2T No 41291 and ex-GWR '57xx' 0-6-0PT No 4666. So popular was the tour that it was repeated on 7 March 1965; together these were two of the last specials to run over former LSWR metals (by now part of the Western Region) in the West Country.

'Britannia' Pacific No 70020 *Mercury* sweeps around the bend into Salisbury station with the Southern Counties Touring Society's 'South Western Rambler' tour of 8 March 1964. The train had already visited Ludgershall behind the locomotive on the truncated remains of the Midland & South Western Junction Railway from Andover to Cheltenham, closed in 1960 but kept open to Ludgershall to serve the military camp at Tidworth. The train then visited the SDJR to Blandford Forum behind a '9F' 2-10-0, No 92209, before returning to Bournemouth. A visit to the Southern Region by a 'Britannia' was a rare occurrence in the 1960s.

SNOW!

In the days following the first LCGB 'S15 Commemorative' railtour of 16 January 1966 with 'S15' No 30837, the weather in southern England turned very cold. By the time of the repeat railtour the landscape was carpeted with snow, so it was decided to use a Class U Mogul, No 31639, as assisting locomotive for the heavily graded Alton–Eastleigh section of the tour. Here the two locomotives are seen doing battle with the 1-in-60 climb from Alton to Medstead. No 31639, then on its third successive weekend of railtour duty, had already headed the special up the Bentley–Bordon branch and back. This relief tour marked the demise of this distinctive Maunsell class.

Preserved Caledonian Single No 123 pauses at Luib on the Caledonian line to Oban on 12 April 1963 — the first day of that year's 'Scottish Rambler' tour (see pages 54-57). It has just fought its way up five miles at 1 in 60 away from Glen Ogle in a snowstorm, only just managing not to slip to a stand. The train would proceed to Crianlarich Upper via the loop on to the West Highland line before returning to Glasgow.

GW TANKS PRESERVED

Left: On 17 October 1965 the SLS 'GWR Cavalcade Special' from Worcester was hauled as far as Gloucester by a pair of ex-GWR locomotives that were already in preservation, '14xx' 0-4-2T No 1420 and '64xx' 0-6-0PT No 6435. Here, No 1420 has come off the train for water at Gloucester South Junction.

Below left: No 6435 takes its turn at the water column before continuing as pilot to No 7029 *Clun Castle* (already also earmarked for preservation) on the run to Bristol. All three locomotives would subsequently go on shed at Bristol St Philips Marsh. This special was used to transfer the two privately preserved tank engines, owned by Pat Whitehouse, to the Dart Valley Railway (nowadays the South Devon Railway).

Right: Pat Whitehouse also owned GWR '45xx' 2-6-2T No 4555, here seen taking water at Tyseley shed on 13 June 1964 before heading the SLS 'West Midlands' special from Birmingham to Bromyard via Stourbridge Junction and Worcester. By this time Bromyard had become the freight-only terminus of a line that once went through to Leominster and branches beyond.

FADING LIGHT

In the last of the afternoon light, Class U 2-6-0 No 61639 pilots the last operational 'Q1', No 33006 on the eastbound climb to Medstead & Four Marks (nowadays the province of the Mid-Hants Railway) with the returning LCGB 'Wilts and Hants' tour from Salisbury via Southampton on 3 April 1966. This was the last occasion on which a 'Q1' was used on a passenger train.

Preserved HR 'Jones Goods' 4-6-0 No 103 and GNSR 4-4-0 No 49 *Gordon Highlander* pause for water at Barrhill in fading light while double-heading the final stage of the 1963 'Scottish Rambler' from Stranraer back to Glasgow, over the Ayrshire moors via Girvan, on 15 April 1963.

SOUTHERN FAREWELL

Above: Steam on the Southern Region finally came to an end on 9 July 1967 with some exciting runs on the Bournemouth line, speeds of up to 100mph being reported by enthusiasts. Here BR Standard Class 5 No 73029 and Light Pacific No 34023 *Blackmore Vale* speed up the 1-in-110 bank from Petersfield to Buriton Tunnel, on the LSWR Guildford–Portsmouth main line, on the first leg of the RCTS 'Farewell to Southern Steam' tour, which they headed as far as Fareham. Run on 18 June, this was the last Society special before the end of steam on the Southern Region. A regular on the Somerset & Dorset line, No 73029 had been allocated to Bath Green Park, latterly a Western Region shed, and would retain its green passenger livery to the end.

Right: Later in the day a pair of Light Pacifics — Nos 34023 *Blackmore Vale* and 34108 *Wincanton* — pound up the 1-in-50 Upwey Bank to Binscombe Tunnels on the RCTS 'Farewell' railtour; they are on their way back from Weymouth to Salisbury, where 'Merchant Navy' No 35103 *Blue Funnel* would take over for the run to Waterloo. With No 34102 *Lapford*, No 34023 was destined to be one of the last two unrebuilt Light Pacifics.

FLYING SCOTSMAN

Above: For its first preserved outing in Alan Pegler's ownership, No 4472 *Flying Scotsman*, rebuilt with single chimney (with no smoke-deflectors) and restored to LNER apple-green livery, hauled the RPS 'Great Central Special' from Sheffield to London via the Great Central route on 15 June 1963. Here No 4472 takes water at Cricklewood shed.

Right: *Flying Scotsman* rests at Basingstoke shed on 10 September 1966 after heading the annual 'Farnborough Flyer' special to the Farnborough Air Show.

'BLACK FIVES' ON TOUR

'Black Five' 4-6-0 No 45305 approaches Burscough Bridge for a photo-stop *en route* to Liverpool Docks with the LCGB 'Lancastrian' railtour of 6 April 1968, which it headed throughout. After the photo-stop the 'Black Five' took the ex-L&Y line to Southport via the coast line to Liverpool docks.

The train had started from Liverpool Lime Street and run via Speke and Northenden Junction to Stockport and Manchester London Road. Nowadays No 45305 is one of the best known of the preserved 'Black Fives' and is seen regularly on the main line.

Immaculate 'Black Five' 4-6-0 No 45156 *Ayrshire Yeomanry* prepares to leave Morecambe Promenade on 20 April 1968 with the second RCTS 'Lancastrian' tour, which it would double-head with another 'Black Five', No 45342, to Heysham Harbour before returning via Morecambe, Hellifield and Blackburn to Preston, where the pair would hand back to 'Britannia' No 70013 *Oliver Cromwell* (see page 106) for the final leg of the journey back to Liverpool.

LAST MONTHS IN THE NORTH WEST

'Black Five' No 44949 and BR Standard Class 5 No 73069 (the last to remain operational) pull away from a photo-stop at Rose Grove *en route* to Preston with the Warwickshire Railway Society 'Farewell to Steam' tour of 18 May 1968. The two locomotives headed the tour from Stockport to Preston via Copy Pit and Darwen, where No 70013 *Oliver Cromwell* took over for the next leg via Blackburn and Hellifield to Morecambe; from there the two Class 5s took the special back to Stockport, electric traction then returning it to Coventry.

Having taken over at Carnforth from 'Britannia' No 70013 *Oliver Cromwell*, Standard Class 4s Nos 75019 and 75027 arrive at Skipton with the MRTS/SVRS 'Farewell to Steam' special of 28 July 1968. They were two of the last five survivors of the class, kept for operating to Swinden Quarry on the Grassington branch at Rylstone, and were maintained in good external condition by enthusiast cleaners. They survived to the end of steam, but although No 75027 was saved for preservation on the Bluebell Railway No 75019 was scrapped in Scotland.

Above: At Skipton the two BR Class 4 locomotives used on the MRTS/SVRS 'Farewell to Steam' tour of 28 July 1968 handed over to 'Black Five' 4-6-0s Nos 45073 and 45156, seen here storming away from Skipton, bound for Rose Grove via a circuitous route that would take in Lostock Hall Junction, Chorley and Bolton.

Right: With the willowherb in full bloom, 'Black Fives' Nos 45073 and 45156 make light work of the climb up to Sough Tunnel, near Entwistle, *en route* from Bolton to Blackburn and Rose Grove with the MRTS/SVRS 'Farewell to Steam' railtour of 28 July 1968. At Rose Grove the last '8F' 2-8-0, No 48773, would take over for the last steam-hauled leg via Copy Pit to Manchester Victoria and Stockport (see page 47).

FINAL FAREWELL

Right: Having worked from Manchester Victoria via Copy Pit, 'Black Fives' Nos 44871 and 44894 storm the southern ascent to Sough Tunnel, near Spring Vale, with the first of the SLS 'Farewell to Steam' specials returning to Birmingham on 4 August 1968 — the day after the cessation of steam haulage in normal service on British Railways.

Below right: A short time later *Oliver Cromwell* pilots 'Black Five' No 44781 down the grade from Sough Tunnel in the other direction with the SLS 'Farewell to Steam' special to Blackburn, where the train would be taken over by '8F' No 48773 piloting the 'Black Five' to Hellifield. A week later these locomotives — and the 'Black Fives' seen in the previous picture — would all participate in the official farewell to main-line BR steam.